PURPLE

by Melanie Mitchell

first step nonfiction

Lerner Publications · Minneapolis

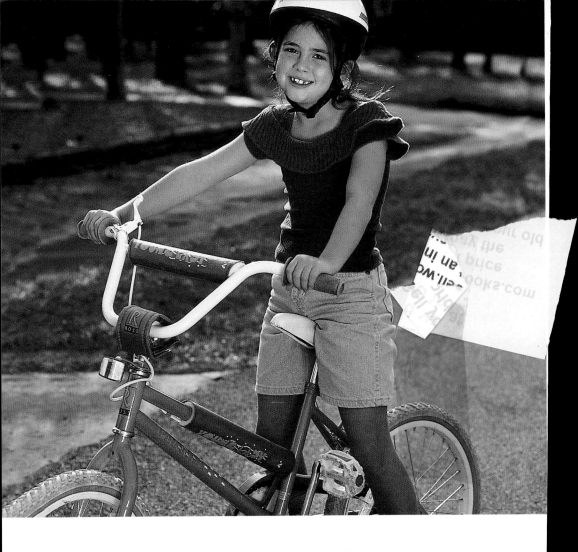

I see purple.

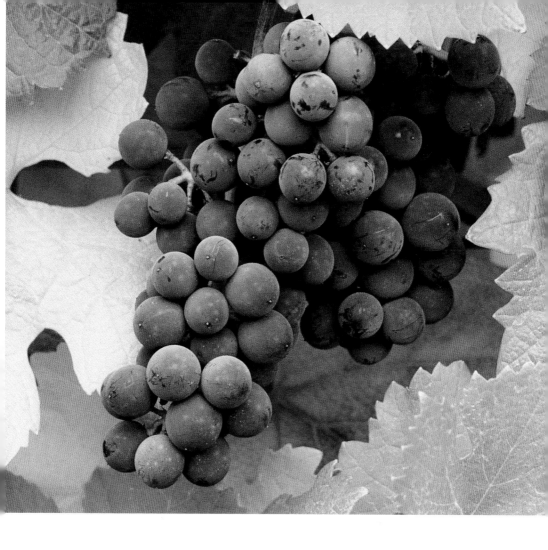

A grape is purple.

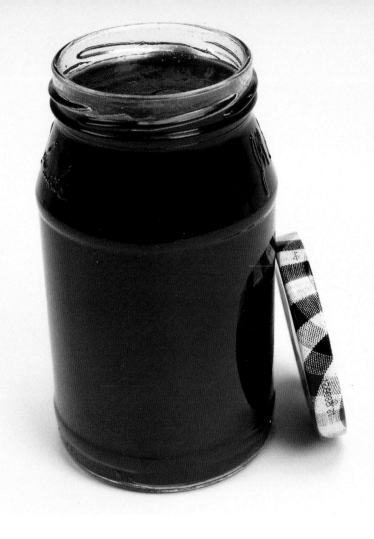

The jelly is purple.

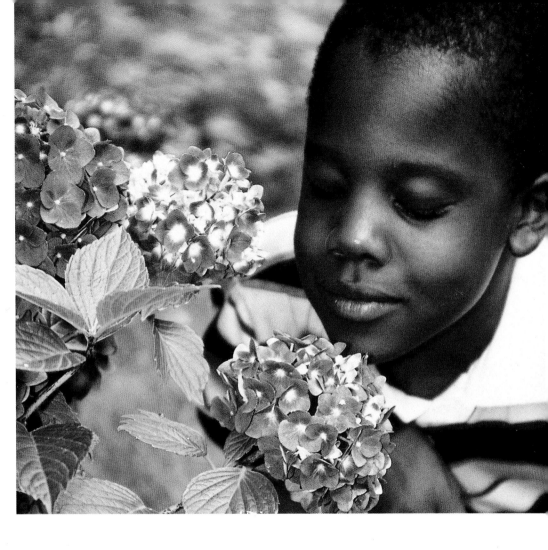

A flower is purple.

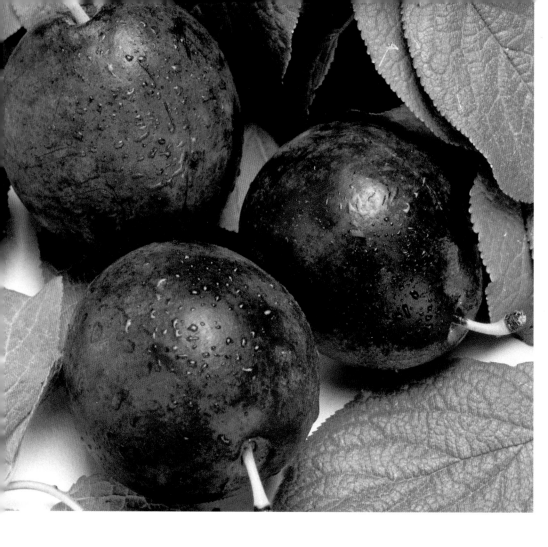

A plum is purple.

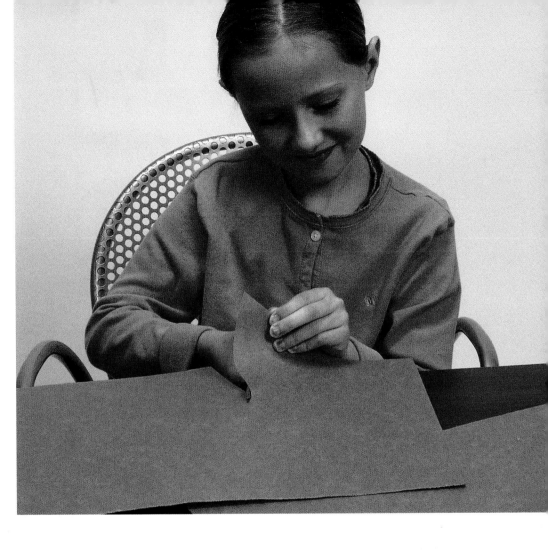

The paper is purple.

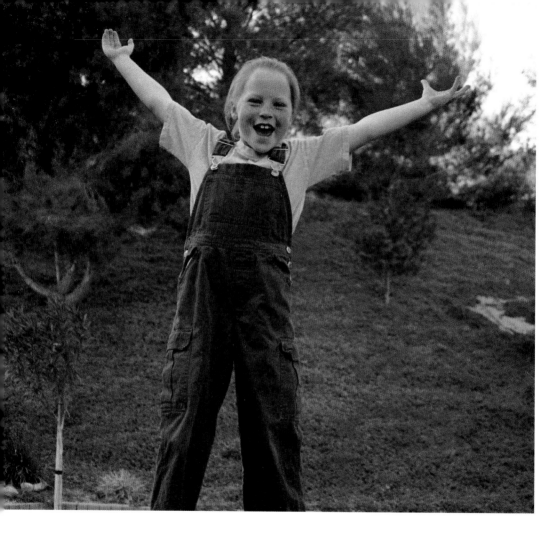

I like purple!